100 Fun WAYS TO QUIT YOUR JOB

Unconventional Ways To Break Free From The Daily Grind

"Thank you for choosing our small publishing company for your literary journey. We greatly appreciate your support, which allows us to continue bringing unique and inspiring stories to readers like you. If you enjoyed this book, please consider leaving a review. Your feedback not only helps fellow readers discover exceptional reads but also supports independent publishers like us in our mission to share captivating stories with the world. We value your input and look forward to hearing your thoughts."

In the world of work, there exists a universal truth: sooner or later, the time comes to say farewell to your job. Whether you're departing for greener pastures, seeking new challenges, or, let's be honest, desperately fleeing from the stifling clutches of your current cubicle, quitting your job is an inevitable part of the professional journey.

But why, oh why, should farewells be mundane, somber affairs filled with awkward handshakes, manila envelopes, and the inescapable feeling that you might have forgotten your favorite coffee mug in the breakroom? Why not, instead, make your exit from the world of nine-to-five a memorable spectacle, a story that will be told around water coolers and virtual Zoom happy hours for years to come?

Ladies and gentlemen, welcome to a collection of real-life tales of resignation like you've never seen before. These stories aren't mere figments of imagination; they're the stuff of workplace legend, based on true events that prove there's no one-size-fits-all approach to quitting your job.

In the pages that follow, you'll meet a cast of characters who took their farewells to unprecedented heights.

They didn't just leave their jobs; they performed Houdini-level vanishing acts, orchestrated elaborate office-wide scavenger hunts, and even enlisted the help of fortune tellers and puppetry to craft their goodbyes.

Yes, these are the tales of individuals who dared to make their exits as unique as the jobs they were leaving behind. They turned their resignations into memorable experiences, complete with humor, creativity, and a dash of audacity.

But be warned, dear reader: as you immerse yourself in these stories, you might find yourself pondering your own exit strategy. Who knows? The next great workplace legend could be authored by you, taking its place among these unforgettable tales.

So, fasten your seatbelts, grab your favorite office chair, and prepare to embark on a journey through the world of unconventional resignations. Whether you're a seasoned professional or just beginning your career, you'll discover that quitting your job can be an art form—one filled with laughter, ingenuity, and, above all, the indomitable spirit to break free from the daily grind.

The Singing Telegram

A musically talented employee hired a singing telegram service to perform a customized resignation song in front of the entire office. The lyrics humorously detailed their reasons for leaving.

Skywriting

An employee hired an airplane to skywrite "I QUIT!" in giant letters above their workplace during a company picnic. Everyone looked up in shock as the message appeared in the sky, and the employee waved goodbye from the airplane.

The Musical Chairs Resignation

During a team-building session, an employee substituted one of the chairs with their resignation letter. When the music stopped, the person who ended up with the letter had to read it aloud.

The Cupcake Farewell

In the vast assembly lines of life, there exists a story that is as heartwarming as it is bittersweet—a tale of a dedicated factory worker who was ready to trade her overalls for a new career journey. Meet Sarah, a tireless soul who had spent long hours on the factory floor, all while pursuing her dream of education by taking night classes.

Sarah's moment of triumph had arrived. She had donned the graduation cap and gown, clutching her hard-earned diploma in hand. It was time to bid farewell to her factory job and embrace the new path she had carved for herself. But Sarah was not one to leave quietly; she chose to express her gratitude in a way that was as thoughtful as it was delicious.

On her last day at the factory, Sarah arrived bearing cupcakes, each one meticulously decorated with a letter. As her coworkers gathered around, they marveled at the sweet treats before them. But it wasn't just the cupcakes that captivated their attention—it was the message that Sarah had spelled out with them.

The cupcakes, when arranged together, formed a message that read, "I must be moving on." It was a heartfelt expression of gratitude and farewell, delivered with the same care and attention to detail that Sarah had shown in her work on the factory floor.

As her colleagues savored the cupcakes, they couldn't help but be moved by Sarah's thoughtfulness. Her gesture was a reminder that even in the midst of transitions, it's essential to acknowledge the support and camaraderie of those who have been part of our journey.

The "Cupcake Farewell" became a cherished memory among Sarah's coworkers. They realized that farewells need not be sad; they can be a celebration of growth, gratitude, and the sweetness of shared experiences.

Sarah's story serves as a reminder that the road to success is often paved with the support and encouragement of those around us. And when it's time to step onto a new path, why not do it with a sweet reminder of the journey that brought us here?

The Office Escape Artist

An employee organized an "Escape Room" challenge in the office. Colleagues had to solve puzzles and riddles to find the exit, which led to the employee's desk with their resignation letter waiting.

The Office Mascot Farewell

Someone who worked with a friendly office dog attached their resignation letter to the dog's collar. As the dog roamed around the office, everyone followed it until they found the message.

The Message in a Bottle Resignation

An employee placed their resignation letter inside a sealed bottle and left it in the breakroom fridge. They sent an email to coworkers with a treasure map leading to the fridge, adding a sense of adventure to their departure.

The Farewell of the First-Grade Maestro

In the heart of an elementary school, amid the laughter and scribbles of young learners, there's a story that resonates with the purest notes of childhood—a tale of a first-grade teacher whose decision to move to a new state marked the end of an era in her classroom.

Meet Mrs. Anderson, the dedicated first-grade maestro who had spent years nurturing the minds and hearts of her young charges. She had become an integral part of the school's tapestry, and her impending departure was met with both tears and excitement from her students.

On her last day of school, Mrs. Anderson had a surprise in store. She had taught her students a sweet song, a tribute to the school and the beloved principal who had always been a guiding star. With anticipation bubbling in the air, she invited the principal into the classroom.

The children eagerly took their places, and to the familiar tune of "Row, Row, Row Your Boat," they began to sing:
"School, school, here we learn,
With friends at every turn.
Reading, writing, singing, too,
We owe it all to you!"

As the notes filled the room, a sense of nostalgia and gratitude washed over the students, the teacher, and even the principal. It was a heartfelt melody, a serenade to the school and the leadership that had made their learning journey a joyful one.

The principal couldn't help but smile as the young voices lifted in harmony. It was a touching moment, a reminder of the profound impact that educators can have on the lives of their students.

Mrs. Anderson's "Melodious Farewell" became a cherished memory for all who were present. It was a reminder that teaching is not just about imparting knowledge; it's about creating moments of connection and celebration.

Her story serves as a testament to the power of music and the lasting bonds formed in the classroom. And as Mrs. Anderson moved to her new state, she carried with her the echoes of a song that would forever resonate in the hearts of her students and colleagues.

The Plumbing Pipe Resignation

A plumber creatively fashioned the words "I quit" using plastic pipes and fittings, leaving the arrangement on their employer's desk to flow into a new career path.

The Stand-Up Comedy Resignation

A budding comedian announced their resignation during an office meeting but did so by delivering a stand-up comedy routine that had everyone laughing. They poked fun at office quirks and ended with a farewell bow.

The Jenga Resignation

An employee brought a Jenga game to the office, and during a staff meeting, they strategically removed a piece that had "I QUIT" written on it. The tower toppled, and the message was revealed.

The Fortune Cookie Resignation

An employee placed a custom-made fortune cookie on each colleague's desk. Inside each cookie was a message that read, "My fortune lies elsewhere. I quit!"

The Sweet Farewell Flavor

An ice cream parlor employee concocted a unique ice cream flavor named "Quit Your Job" and offered it to customers, delivering her resignation message in a deliciously unconventional way.

The "Stitching My Exit" Gesture

In the vast tapestry of job resignations, there's a thread of creativity that weaves its way into the hearts of those who dare to leave in a truly unique fashion. This is the story of a woman, a seamstress by trade, who chose to bid adieu to her sewing factory job with a gesture that was as skillful as it was heartfelt.

Meet Emma, a dedicated worker who had spent countless hours meticulously sewing garments on the factory floor. Over time, however, she began to feel as though she was stitching herself into a pattern she couldn't break free from. But Emma was not one to leave quietly; she decided to craft her resignation in a way that would leave a lasting impression.

Emma's choice was clear: she would sew her resignation letter, quite literally, into the fabric of her farewell. With nimble fingers and a sense of purpose, she set to work on a plain, white shirt. The thread danced through the fabric, and slowly but surely, the words "I QUIT" began to take shape, embroidered with precision and care.

As Emma presented the finished shirt to her boss, their eyes widened with surprise and admiration. The words, delicately woven into the fabric, were a testament to her skill and her decision to set her own course in life. It was a message that couldn't be ignored or misunderstood.

Emma's coworkers watched in awe as her boss received the handmade resignation shirt. It was a powerful symbol of empowerment, a reminder that we have the ability to craft our own destinies, even when it's time to leave behind what we've known.

The "Stitching My Exit" gesture became legendary in the factory. Emma's colleagues celebrated her creativity and courage. They realized that sometimes, the most powerful farewells are the ones that allow us to express ourselves fully and authentically.

Emma's story serves as a reminder that our jobs are but a single thread in the fabric of our lives. And when it's time to move on, why not sew our exit with the threads of our own aspirations?

The Supermarket Intercom Exit

A supermarket employee used the store's intercom system to announce that assistance was needed at register three. Upon arrival, coworkers discovered her resignation message, broadcasted to all within the store.

The Magician's Disappearing Act

A magician used his skills to turn himself invisible during a team meeting. When his boss called on him to give an update, he remained silent, and eventually, a smoke bomb went off, leaving behind only his resignation letter.

The "Smile and Sign Off" IT Departure

In the world of IT, where codes and cables often take center stage, there exists a story that transcends the binary realm—a tale of an IT professional who chose to log out of his job with a memorable flourish. Meet Jake, a tech-savvy genius who had tirelessly tended to the digital needs of a large company.

Jake's decision to part ways with his IT role was not just an ordinary resignation; it was a tech-savvy swan song. He had spent years working tirelessly behind the scenes, and now, it was time to make his exit with a touch of digital magic.

One fateful day, as Jake sat in his command center, surrounded by rows of computers, he hatched a plan. With a few clicks of the mouse, he changed the screen background on every computer in the office. There, grinning back at each bewildered user, was Jake's own smiling face, accompanied by the words, "Thanks for the memories."

As employees across the office powered up their computers, they were met with an unexpected and slightly eerie sight. Jake's face, radiating a warm smile, greeted them like a digital guardian angel. It was a farewell message that was impossible to ignore, simultaneously puzzling and endearing.

Jake's colleagues couldn't help but chuckle at the audacity and creativity of his exit strategy. As they shared stories of their IT savior turned digital prankster, the office buzzed with laughter and nostalgia.

The "Smile and Sign Off" IT departure became a symbol of Jake's technical prowess and his ability to inject humor into even the most mundane of tasks. It was a reminder that in the digital age, a well-placed smile can leave an indelible mark on the workplace.

Jake's story reminds us that even in the world of technology, where algorithms and data rule, there's always room for a touch of humanity and humor. And when it's time to unplug from one chapter of our lives, why not do it with a smile and a fond farewell?

The Impersonator Quit

A coworker threw an impromptu office costume party, where they dressed as a famous movie character. During the party, they revealed their resignation message in the form of a movie quote.

The T-Shirt Rack Resignation

A young clothing store employee designed a t-shirt with "I quit" boldly printed on it and strategically placed it on a rack of shirts for their employer to discover, using fashion to bid farewell.

The Artistic Exit

A graphic designer created a series of funny and satirical cartoons depicting their workplace frustrations and why they were leaving. They posted these cartoons all over the office for coworkers to discover.

The Pizza Party Farewell

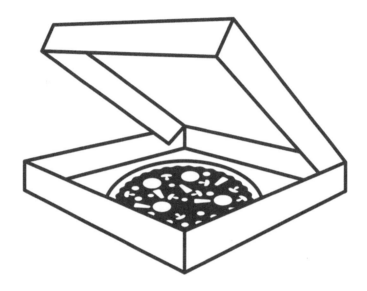

A man working in a small accounting firm hosted a pizza party for his coworkers. Little did they know that at the bottom of the pizza box lay his resignation message, delivering the news with a slice of humor.

The Pie and a Side of Resignation

In the annals of unconventional job resignations, there's a tale that's as sweet as pie – quite literally. Picture this: a bustling diner, the clatter of plates, and a waitress who decided it was high time to bid farewell in a way that left everyone with a taste of wonder.

Our protagonist, let's call her Sarah, had spent years dishing out delicious pies and taking orders at that very diner. But, as fate would have it, the time for her to cut a different slice of life arrived. And oh, did she do it in style.

One fine afternoon, Sarah sauntered up to her boss, order slip in hand. The slip bore a seemingly typical request: "Two slices of pie." But as her boss read on, they discovered an unexpected surprise: "And oh yes, I quit."

As the order slip made its way through the kitchen, it sparked a flurry of whispers, giggles, and raised eyebrows. The customers craned their necks to catch a glimpse of the waitress who had turned her resignation into a culinary masterpiece.

You see, Sarah knew that farewells, much like pie, should be memorable and leave a sweet aftertaste. Her choice to blend her resignation with a slice of humor showcased her unique spirit and added a dash of flavor to an otherwise ordinary workday.

In that quaint diner, Sarah's pie and a side of resignation became the stuff of legend, a reminder that sometimes, the most extraordinary farewells come in the humblest of forms. Her colleagues may have missed her warm smile and efficient service, but they'll forever savor the memory of that unforgettable order slip.

And as for Sarah, well, she went on to pursue her dreams, knowing that her slice of life could be whatever flavor she desired. Her tale reminds us that, much like pie, our careers are meant to be savored and sometimes spiced up with a touch of audacity.

The Popsicle Stick House Quit

A resourceful receptionist in a real estate office built a tiny house from popsicle sticks and left it on the boss's desk, accompanied by a miniature sign declaring her departure with whimsical charm.

The "Wooden Resignation" Blueprint

In the world of construction, where every structure begins with a solid foundation, there's a tale of a worker who decided to build his own path to freedom, one wooden plank at a time. Meet Dave, a hardworking soul who had had enough of his overbearing boss, a master of excuses when it came to docking paychecks.

Dave had spent countless hours under the sun, laying bricks, pouring concrete, and enduring his boss's relentless demands. But there comes a point when even the strongest foundation begins to crack, and Dave decided it was time to construct his own exit strategy, quite literally.

One fateful morning, armed with a vision and a handful of 2x4s, Dave set to work. He meticulously framed each letter, taking care to ensure the lines were straight and the angles were precise. He knew that this wooden canvas would be the blueprint for his grand departure.

As the sun reached its zenith, Dave stepped back to admire his handiwork. The wooden letters spelled out a message that was as clear as day: "I QUIT."

With a sense of accomplishment, Dave nailed the letters together, forming a solid declaration of his decision. The structure of his resignation was sound, built to withstand even the harshest criticism from his boss.

When the time came to deliver his message, Dave didn't need a lengthy speech or a dramatic exit. He simply left his wooden creation in a place where his boss couldn't miss it. As the boss read those bold, wooden letters, there was a moment of stunned silence, followed by a realization that Dave had crafted his own exit strategy with the same precision and dedication that he brought to his work every day.

Dave's "Wooden Resignation" became the stuff of legend at the construction site. It was a testament to his craftsmanship, his determination, and his refusal to let anyone diminish his worth. His coworkers cheered him on as he walked away from that job site, knowing that Dave had not only built structures but had also constructed his own path to freedom.

Dave's story reminds us that sometimes, in the face of an overbearing boss, the best way to make a statement is to build it yourself. Whether it's with bricks or with wooden planks, our resignations can be as solid and unshakable as the foundations we've laid in our careers.

The Dancing Exit

A passionate dancer choreographed a dance routine to a popular song and performed it in the middle of the office as their resignation announcement. Coworkers joined in, and it turned into an impromptu dance party.

The Decorative Dustpan Resignation

A house cleaner expressed her resignation by presenting her employer with a creatively decorated dustpan. The message was clear: she was sweeping herself away from the job.

The Boxception Resignation

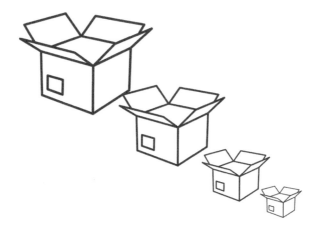

An office worker sent their employer a series of nested boxes, with ten boxes in total. Inside the smallest box, a tiny note revealed their resignation, adding an element of surprise and intrigue.

The Windshield Resignation

A car salesman left his boss a message they couldn't miss. Using a window marker, he wrote "I quit" on the windshield of a car, making sure his resignation was in the driver's seat of his career decisions.

The Cake Resignation

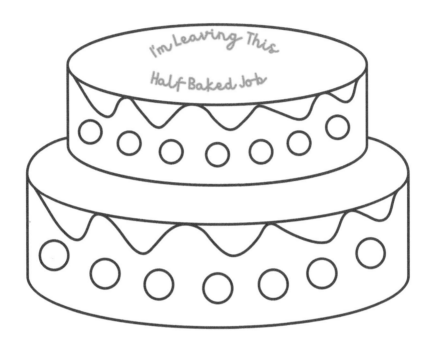

A baker decided to quit her job by making a beautifully decorated cake that said, "I'm leaving this half-baked job." She presented it to her boss and walked out with a slice in hand.

The Hula-Hoop Resignation

A fitness enthusiast used a hula-hoop performance as their resignation method. They gathered their coworkers in a common area and hula-hooped while explaining why they were leaving.

The Office Prankster's Resignation

A known office prankster sent an email to the entire company with a subject line that said, "Important Announcement." When employees opened the email, they found a video of the prankster dancing joyfully while holding their resignation letter.

The Soapy Departure

In the realm of unconventional job resignations, there's a story that truly cleans up the competition – and it's all about a window washer who saw the opportunity to write his own exit strategy in a most unexpected canvas: the grime-covered windows of his boss's office.

Meet Tom, a dedicated window washer who had scaled the heights of skyscrapers and conquered every streaked pane that dared to challenge him. But in every profession, there comes a time when even the clearest of glass reveals cracks in the workplace foundation.

Tom had been working under the watchful eye of his boss, a persnickety individual who never missed a chance to scrutinize the cleanliness of every window. Yet, as Tom peered through the panes day after day, he couldn't help but feel that he was laboring under conditions that were far from crystal clear.

One fateful morning, as he stood outside his boss's office, squeegee in hand, Tom had a revelation. Instead of removing the grime, he could use it to deliver his message. With the same precision he used to achieve spotless windows, he began to etch his resignation into the dirt.

Letter by letter, word by word, Tom's message took shape on the office window. The words "I QUIT" emerged as a stark contrast against the filth that had accumulated on the glass. It was a resignation letter like no other, a testament to his resourcefulness and the creativity that can blossom even in the most mundane of tasks.

As the boss entered the office, their eyes widened in disbelief. The message was unmissable, impossible to ignore. Tom had used the very grime he had battled against for so long to deliver a message that was as clear as day.

The boss, though undoubtedly frustrated, couldn't help but admire the audacity of Tom's exit strategy. In a way, it was a work of art, a reminder that even in the midst of dirty work, there's room for creativity and self-expression.

Tom's "Soapy Departure" became a legend among his fellow window washers and served as a symbol of ingenuity in the face of a less-than-ideal work environment. With his message etched in grime, he walked away from that office, leaving behind not just a clean window but a lasting impression of his resilience and wit.

The Scavenger Hunt Resignation

This person organized an elaborate office-wide scavenger hunt that led their coworkers to various clues, with the final one being their resignation letter hidden in a clever spot.

The Post-It Note Farewell

An employee covered their entire workspace with colorful Post-It notes, each containing a message or reason for leaving. The result was a visually striking and memorable resignation display.

The Movie Poster Quit

An avid movie buff designed a movie poster featuring themselves as the star and their job as the movie title, with a tagline like "One Last Exit." They hung these posters around the office.

The Cinnamon Roll Parting Gift

A mall security guard presented his employer with a boxed cinnamon roll. On the box, a sweet resignation message was written, combining a delicious treat with his departure announcement.

The Office Garden Resignation

A plant lover gifted each colleague a potted plant with a small card that had their resignation message attached. The plants served as a lasting reminder of their time at the company.

The Balloon Bouquet Quit

An employee handed out helium balloons to coworkers, each with a message inside that collectively spelled out, "I'm flying away from this job." The balloons filled the office with laughter as they floated to the ceiling.

The Office Flash Mob Quit

An outgoing employee organized a surprise flash mob during lunch break. As the music started playing, coworkers joined in a choreographed dance that ended with the resigning employee dramatically walking away.

The Office Zookeeper Farewell

A zookeeper who worked at an animal sanctuary presented their resignation letter by arranging for exotic animals to deliver it. Colleagues were greeted by a parrot carrying a scroll with the message.

The Office Time Capsule Resignation

An employee organized a "time capsule" event where everyone was encouraged to place a message or item in a box. When they opened the capsule, it contained the resigning employee's farewell letter.

The Mime Resignation

A former drama student used mime techniques to silently act out their resignation during a team meeting. Their colleagues had to guess the message, leading to laughter when they finally understood.

The Crossword Puzzle Quit

An employee created a crossword puzzle with clues related to their time at the company. The answers spelled out their resignation message, which they handed out to coworkers.

The Office "Taste Test" Resignation

An employee organized a "taste test" event where coworkers sampled various foods representing their experiences at the company. The final dish revealed their resignation message.

The Fortune Teller Resignation

An employee hired a fortune teller to set up a booth in the office during a company party. When colleagues visited the booth, the fortune teller revealed the employee's resignation in a comically dramatic fashion.

The Rube Goldberg Resignation

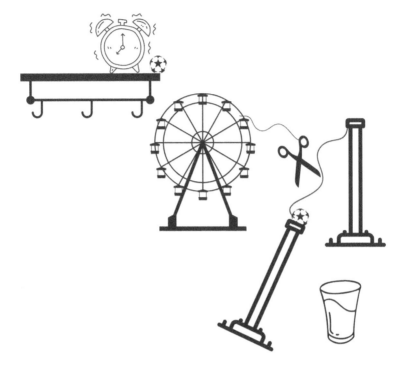

A creative engineer designed an elaborate Rube Goldberg machine that, when activated, triggered a series of chain reactions that ultimately unveiled their resignation letter in an unexpected way.

The Office Detective Farewell

An employee turned their resignation into a detective mystery. They left clues around the office, leading their coworkers on a "case" to uncover the reason behind their departure.

The Coffee Cup Resignation

A coffee enthusiast had custom coffee cups made for each coworker with their resignation message printed at the bottom. As colleagues finished their coffee, they discovered the surprise message.

The Office Karaoke Resignation

A karaoke enthusiast organized an impromptu karaoke session during a company party. They chose a song with fitting lyrics to announce their resignation and belted it out to the surprise of their coworkers.

The Puzzle Master Farewell

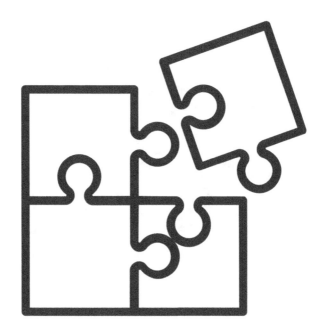

An employee distributed puzzle pieces to their colleagues over a week. Each piece contained a part of their resignation message. On the final day, everyone assembled the puzzle to reveal the message.

The Movie Trailer Resignation

A film buff created a movie trailer-style video announcing their resignation. They used dramatic music, epic narration, and clips from their time at the company to build anticipation.

The Office Art Installation Quit

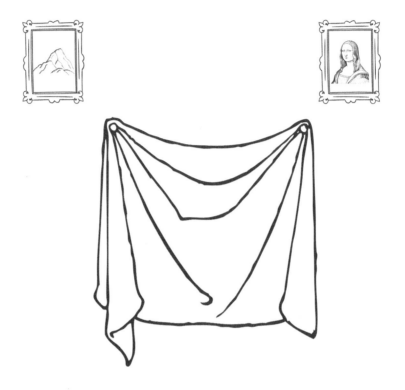

An artist turned their workspace into a mini art gallery, displaying paintings and sculptures that symbolized their journey at the company. Their resignation was unveiled as the centerpiece.

The Video Game Resignation

A gamer employee designed a custom video game where coworkers had to complete challenges related to the workplace. Upon completing the game, they received a message about the employee's departure.

The Escape Pod Resignation

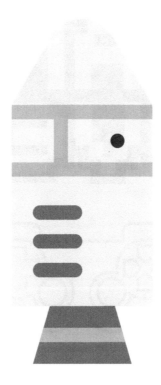

A sci-fi fan constructed a makeshift "escape pod" in their office, complete with blinking lights and sound effects. On their last day, they climbed inside and "launched" themselves out of the company.

The Office Olympics Resignation

 An athletic employee organized an "Office Olympics" event with quirky games related to the workplace. After the games, they revealed their resignation letter on the winner's podium.

The Stand-Up Whiteboard Farewell

A clever individual used a whiteboard to write their resignation in the style of a stand-up comedy routine. They left the whiteboard in a common area for everyone to enjoy.

The Desk Safari Resignation

A departing employee staged a series of humorous photos featuring them "interacting" with office supplies and equipment, creating a desk safari adventure that ended with their resignation message.

The Message in a Balloon Resignation

Colleagues received helium balloons with strings attached. At a designated time, everyone popped their balloons to reveal a confetti-filled message announcing the resignation.

The Office DJ Departure

An employee who was also a DJ organized a surprise "office dance party" during lunchtime. They played energetic music and, as the grand finale, announced their resignation on the mic.

The Custom Comic Book Quit

A talented artist created a personalized comic book that chronicled their journey at the company in a humorous and exaggerated way. They distributed copies to their coworkers as their resignation letter.

The Office Mascot Redux

In a continuation of the "office mascot" theme, an employee dressed up in a quirky costume as they made their resignation announcement, leaving everyone with a memorable image.

The Office Podcast Resignation

An employee with podcasting skills recorded a special episode for the company podcast, where they humorously discussed their decision to leave and shared memorable workplace anecdotes.

The Office Photo Album Farewell

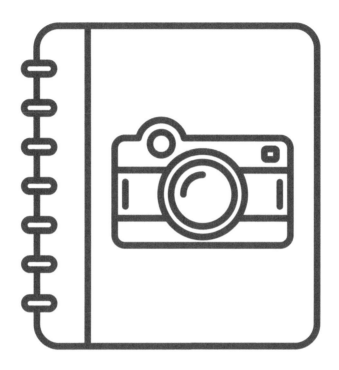

A departing employee compiled a photo album filled with candid and humorous pictures taken around the office over the years. Each photo was captioned with witty comments and anecdotes.

The T-shirt Resignation

The resigning employee designed custom T-shirts for everyone in the office with a witty slogan or message related to their departure. They all wore the shirts on the last day.

The Message in a Bottle, Part 2

A departing colleague placed their resignation letter in a sealed bottle, along with a small ship model. They left it in a decorative "ocean" (a large container of blue water) for coworkers to discover.

The Office Picnic Resignation

An employee organized an office picnic for their farewell. During the picnic, they revealed their resignation message by writing it on a giant banner attached to a kite that soared into the sky.

The "X Bar" Exit

In the world of job resignations, there's a story that's as sweet as it is unique—a tale of a woman who decided to turn her passion for confectionery into her own path to success. Meet Lucy, a dedicated employee at a candy factory where she'd spent years wrapping sugary treats and dreaming of her own candy-making business.

Lucy's decision to leave her job was not just a farewell; it was the birth of a new dream. With unwavering determination, she embarked on a journey to create her own candy empire, one delectable treat at a time. But she didn't just walk out the factory doors; she left on a sweet note—one that would be remembered for years to come.

As a parting gift to her coworkers, Lucy crafted a special candy bar, which she aptly named "The X Bar." She put her heart and soul into the recipe, ensuring it was a harmonious blend of flavors, a reflection of her love for all things sweet.

But Lucy's farewell gesture didn't stop at the candy itself. She took her resignation letter to a whole new level by inscribing it on the candy bar's wrapper. It read, "I Quit," in elegant, swirling letters, a message as sweet as the treat it enveloped.

The day Lucy distributed her homemade "X Bars" marked a bittersweet moment for her coworkers. They marveled at her talent, tasted her creation, and were touched by her creativity. Lucy had managed to combine her farewell with her passion, leaving behind not just a job but a legacy of sweetness.

The "X Bar" exit, as it came to be known, became a symbol of pursuing one's dreams and crafting a future filled with the things you love. Lucy's coworkers cherished the candy bars, not just for their delicious taste but for the reminder that sometimes, the sweetest farewells are the ones that lead to new beginnings.

Lucy's story reminds us that our jobs, like candy, are meant to be enjoyed and savored. And when it's time to move on, why not do it with a touch of sweetness and a dream in your pocket?

The Musical Serenade Resignation

A musically inclined worker recruited a local band to serenade their coworkers with a personalized song that humorously recounted their time at the company while announcing their departure.

The Office Documentary Quit:

A departing employee with video production skills created a mockumentary-style video about the "office jungle." The video featured humorous interviews with coworkers and concluded with their resignation.

The Office Game Show Resignation

The resigning colleague hosted a mock game show during a company event, where participants answered trivia questions related to office culture. The final question unveiled the resignation message.

The Office Yearbook Farewell

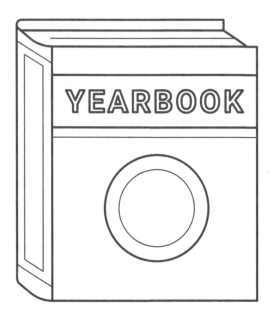

A departing colleague designed an office yearbook filled with photos, quotes, and funny memories from their time at the company. They distributed copies to coworkers as their farewell gesture.

The Office Relay Resignation

The resigning employee organized an office relay race that took participants on a tour of significant locations within the workplace, with the final leg leading to the revelation of their resignation letter.

The Office Balloon Drop Quit

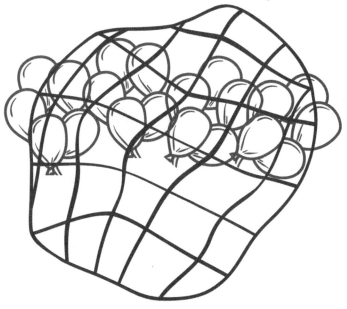

At a surprise office party, the employee rigged the ceiling with a net full of balloons. When they announced their resignation, they pulled a cord, releasing the balloons and their resignation message.

The Custom Comic Strip Farewell

An artistic employee created a series of comic strips featuring office caricatures and inside jokes, leading up to a final strip where they announced their departure.

*The Office Mystery Resignation

The departing employee designed a "mystery box" challenge that involved solving puzzles and riddles related to their decision to leave. The final puzzle unveiled their resignation message.

The Office Cookbook Quit

An employee with a passion for cooking created a custom office cookbook filled with recipes for their favorite dishes. The last page contained their resignation message, leaving coworkers with a culinary keepsake.

The Office Bingo Resignation

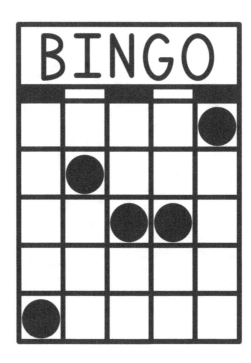

The resigning employee handed out bingo cards to colleagues with humorous workplace scenarios. During a farewell meeting, they called out the scenarios until someone shouted "Bingo!" and their resignation was revealed.

The Office Fashion Show Farewell

An employee who loved fashion organized a runway-style fashion show during a company event. They walked down the "catwalk" wearing different outfits representing their time at the company, ending with their resignation attire.

The Office Time Travel Resignation

An imaginative worker created a "time machine" in the breakroom. During a farewell gathering, they pretended to activate it and announced their resignation while acting like they were traveling to the future.

The Office Improv Resignation:

An employee with a background in improv comedy organized an impromptu comedy skit during a team meeting. They incorporated their resignation into the skit, adding humor to their farewell.

The Office Museum Resignation

A history enthusiast transformed their workspace into a mini museum, showcasing artifacts, memorabilia, and humorous exhibits related to their time at the company. Their resignation letter was displayed as the centerpiece.

The Office TED Talk Farewell

A confident speaker delivered a TED Talk-style presentation during a team meeting, sharing insights and humorous anecdotes from their job. They concluded by announcing their resignation as the grand finale.

The Office Spy Resignation

The departing employee created a playful "spy mission" for their coworkers. Participants had to follow a series of clues that led to their resignation letter hidden in a top-secret file.

The Office Origami Quit

A coworker with origami skills folded intricate origami creations for each colleague. When unfolded, each piece revealed a part of their resignation message, creating a beautiful and surprising display.

The Office Space Mission Farewell

A resigning employee created an elaborate "space launch" experience within their office, complete with countdowns and faux blast-offs, culminating in their resignation announcement.

The "Mowing Forward" Resignation

In the world of landscaping, where nature's beauty meets human creativity, there exists a story that's a cut above the rest—a tale of a determined landscaper who decided to sculpt his resignation in a way that was both unconventional and undeniably green. Meet Mike, a diligent worker who had spent years tending to gardens, shaping lawns, and sculpting landscapes.

Mike had reached a crossroads in his career, where the urge to embark on a new adventure beckoned him. He had decided to bid adieu to his job, but he wanted to do it in a way that paid homage to his love for landscaping. And so, he hatched a plan that was as green as the grass he'd meticulously cared for.

One sunny morning, armed with a lawnmower and a vision, Mike set to work on a sprawling lawn. As the lawnmower roared to life, it traced a path that would soon reveal his heartfelt message. With each carefully calculated pass, the grass was mowed into the words "I QUIT," clearly etched against the sea of green.

Once Mike had completed his grassy masterpiece, he stepped back to admire his handiwork. From above, it was a message that could be seen with utmost clarity, a resignation that was as bold as it was unconventional.

Mike didn't stop at the lawn, though. He snapped a photograph of his creation and sent it to his boss, delivering his resignation with a touch of artistic flair. His boss, upon receiving the message, couldn't help but admire Mike's ingenuity, even as they bid farewell to a valued employee.

The "Mowing Forward" resignation was a testament to Mike's dedication to his craft and his desire to move forward with a sense of boldness and creativity. It was a reminder that even in the most unexpected of places, there's room for self-expression and artistry.

Mike's story serves as an inspiration to embrace our passions when bidding farewell to one chapter of our lives. And as he walked away from that lawn, he left behind not just a message but a vivid reminder that the beauty of life lies in our ability to shape it, even in our goodbyes.

The Office Game Night Resignation

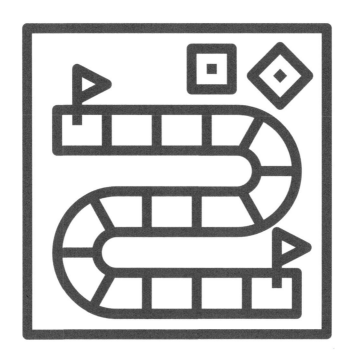

A board game enthusiast organized an "office game night" event. Among the board games was a custom-made game that, when played, unveiled their resignation message on the game board.

The Office Magician's Vanishing Act:

A magician employee incorporated their resignation into their magic act during a company event. They appeared to vanish into thin air, leaving behind only a briefcase with their resignation letter inside.

The Office Haiku Resignation

An employee with a knack for poetry sent out a series of haikus to their colleagues over the course of a week. The haikus subtly conveyed their decision to leave and their fond memories of the workplace.

The Office Puppet Show Quit:

A coworker skilled in puppetry hosted an office puppet show, with the puppets acting out humorous scenarios from the workplace. The grand finale featured the puppets announcing the employee's resignation.

The Office Comedy Roast Farewel

A good-humored colleague organized an office "comedy roast" event. Coworkers took turns delivering light-hearted roasts about the resigning employee, who joined in with their own funny anecdotes before revealing their departure.

The Office Impressionist Resignation

An employee who excelled at celebrity impressions performed a series of entertaining impersonations during a company party. They concluded by announcing their resignation in the voice of a famous figure.

The "Mission Impossible" Resignation

The resigning employee created an office-wide "Mission Impossible" scenario, complete with secret agent props and tasks. Solving the mission eventually led coworkers to the announcement of their departure.

The Office Spelling Bee Farewell

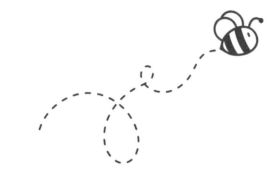

Chrysanthemum

An employee hosted an office spelling bee competition, where participants had to spell words related to their job and the company culture. The final word they had to spell was their resignation message.

The Office Book Club Resignation

An avid reader who loved literature organized an "office book club" meeting. Instead of discussing a book, they distributed personalized short stories that humorously narrated their journey at the company, ending with their resignation.

The Office Jeopardy Resignation

The resigning colleague hosted an office-wide game of "Jeopardy!" with categories related to their job and the workplace. The final jeopardy question revealed their resignation message.

The Office Lip Sync Battle Quit

An employee organized an office lip sync battle, complete with costume changes and dramatic performances. They closed the event by delivering their resignation announcement through a lip-synced song.

The Office Robot Resignation

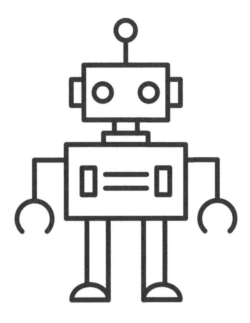

A tech-savvy employee created a small robot that roamed the office with a tablet screen displaying their farewell message. Coworkers followed the robot until they read the message.

The Office LEGO Resignation

A LEGO enthusiast constructed a miniature office scene with LEGO bricks, complete with tiny figurines of coworkers. The scene included a LEGO figure holding a tiny resignation letter.

The Lovely Garden Resignation

An employee transformed a neglected office garden into a vibrant, blooming space. The resignation message was cleverly concealed within the arrangement of flowers and plants.

Conclusion: "A Farewell to Remember

As we reach the final chapter of this collection, it's only fitting to reflect on the whirlwind of creativity and humor that has surrounded us. We've ventured through tales of grand escapades, office magic shows, and even the occasional puppetry performance—all in the name of saying goodbye to the workplace.

What these stories have shown us is that a job resignation need not be a somber affair. It can be a canvas upon which we paint our personalities, our quirks, and our unique perspectives. It's a chance to remind ourselves and those around us that work is not just about deadlines and meetings; it's also about the people, the laughter, and the shared experiences that make the journey worthwhile.

While these tales may have pushed the boundaries of convention, they all share a common thread: they were born from the desire to leave a lasting impression, to create a farewell that colleagues would talk about for years to come. They remind us that life is too short for monotony, and our time at work should be filled with moments of genuine connection, inspiration, and, yes, even a touch of absurdity.

So, as you close the book on this collection of unconventional resignations, I encourage you to take with you the spirit of these stories. When the time comes for you to bid adieu to your own cubicle, remember that you have the power to craft a farewell that reflects your personality, your passions, and your sense of humor.

Let these tales serve as a reminder that in the grand narrative of our lives, the moments that stand out are often the ones that defy convention, the ones that make us laugh, and the ones that remind us of the unique human beings we are. After all, our jobs may come and go, but the stories we create along the way, those are the true treasures of our careers.

So here's to the art of the extraordinary exit, to quitting with flair, and to making our farewells truly unforgettable. After all, as the saying goes, "It's not 'goodbye'; it's 'see you later,' with a twist."

Made in United States
Cleveland, OH
16 December 2024

12001397R00066